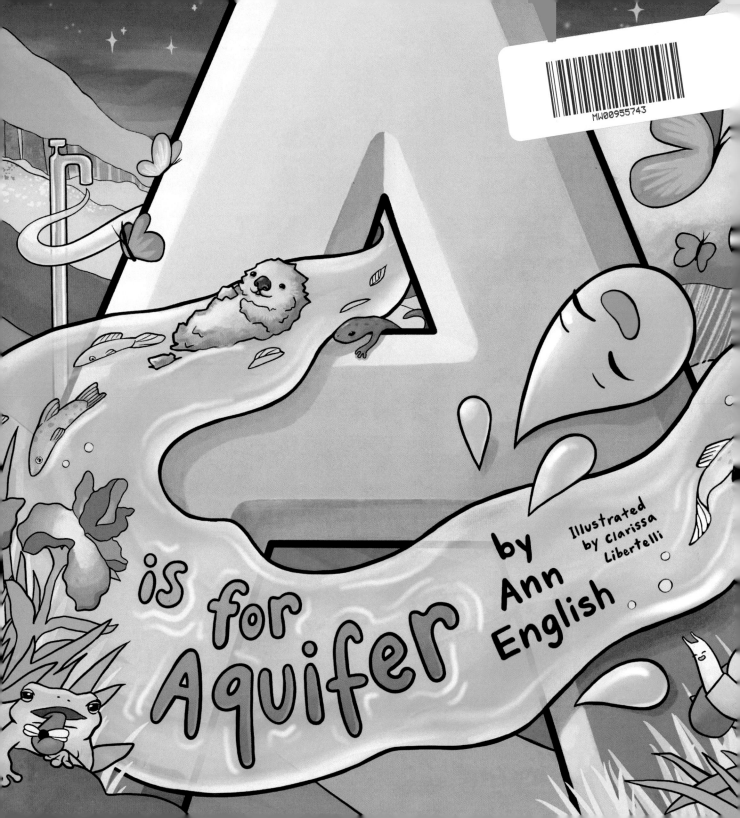

A

is for Aquifer

by Ann English

Illustrated by Clarissa Libertelli

A is for Aquifer
Copyright © 2021 Ann English

Produced and printed by Stillwater River Publications.
All rights reserved. Written and produced
in the United States of America.

Visit our website at
www.StillwaterPress.com
for more information.

First Stillwater River Publications Edition

ISBN: 978-1-955123-74-7

Library of Congress Control Number: 2021925731

12345678910
Written by Ann English
Illustrated by Clarissa Libertelli
Published by Stillwater River Publications,
Pawtucket, RI, USA.

Publisher's Cataloging-In-Publication Data
(Prepared by The Donohue Group, Inc.)

Names: English, Ann, 1958- author. | Libertelli, Clarissa, illustrator.
Title: A is for aquifer / by Ann English ; illustrated by Clarissa Libertelli.
Description: First Stillwater River Publications edition. | Pawtucket, RI, USA : Stillwater
River Publications, [2022] | Interest age level: 005-010. | Includes bibliographical
references. | Summary: "A is for Aquifer is an alphabet book that features life and water
relationships. Rhymes and drawings take the reader on a ... journey through the water
cycle and reveal how what is invisible (groundwater in the aquifer) becomes visible and
available ... with each letter"-- Provided by publisher.
Identifiers: ISBN 9781955123730
Subjects: LCSH: Hydrologic cycle--Juvenile literature. | English
language--Alphabet--Juvenile literature. | CYAC: Hydrologic cycle. | English
language--Alphabet. | LCGFT: Alphabet books.
Classification: LCC GB848 .E54 2022 | DDC 551.48--dc23

A is for Aquifer

I love alphabet books—but I discovered that although there were many clever books with many versions of the alphabet, there were none specifically focused on water. Since I work with water all of the time, this seemed like an amazing omission to me. And so the first verse came, and then B, and then the serious effort began.

I was fortunate to have a great collaborator to work with, once I had the basic text prepared. Clarissa Libertelli brought my words and thought sketches into richly colored visuals that are both fun to look at and illustrate the words' meaning. I want to thank my friends and colleagues who encouraged me and gave me their honest feedback that this sounded like a book they wanted to see! Thanks too, to my husband Don, who has always believed that if I set my mind to something I can accomplish it.

So, "Why this book?" In part, because we all need clean water . . . and fun words to learn. If young children can learn about dinosaurs and go on to become paleontologists, then if they learn about water, perhaps they will find ways to remember its importance as they grow up. This book is especially for Meredith and Arthur; my hope is that "clean water for all" comes closer to reality in their lifetimes.

- Ann English

A is for Aquifer, where groundwater runs deep. Hydraulically connected formations intersect the Earth's surface in seeps.

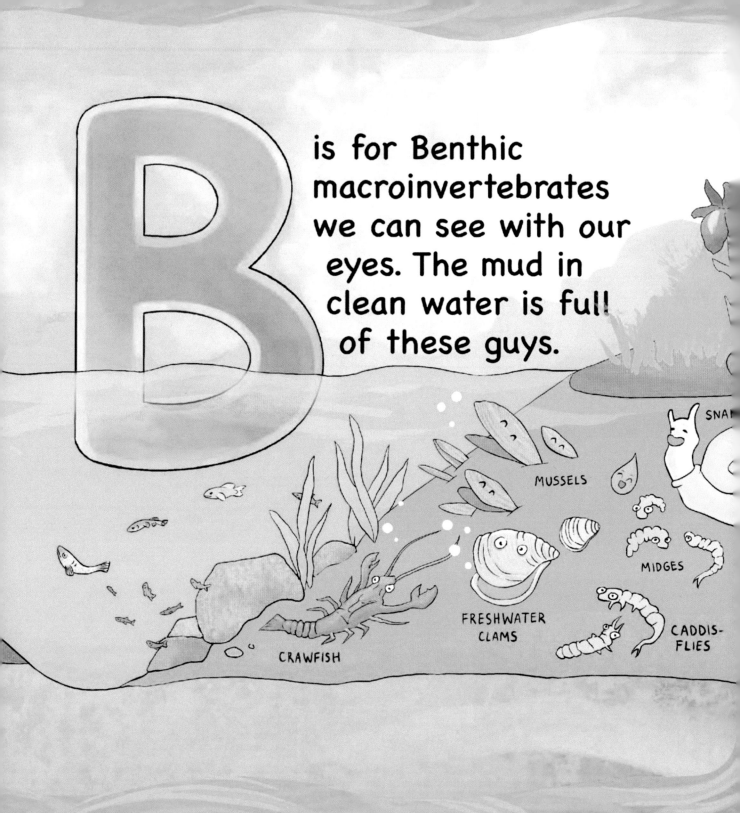

is for Benthic macroinvertebrates we can see with our eyes. The mud in clean water is full of these guys.

CRAWFISH

FRESHWATER CLAMS

MUSSELS

SNA[IL]

MIDGES

CADDIS-FLIES

C is for Conservation landscapes and more. Clean water starts at home, just outside your door.

D is for Downpour, like a summer rain. Special gardens and pavements keep pollution from the drains.

E is for Estuaries, where water meets the sea, an abundance of life growing wild and free.

F is for Fish, swimming in streams. If we find lots of diversity, we know the water is clean.

BLUE RIDGE SCULPIN

NORTHERN HOGSUCKER

GREENSIDE DARTER

GREEN SUNFISH

BROWN TROUT

AMERICAN EEL

CREEK CHUB

BROWN BULLHEAD

BLACK NOSE DACE

G is for Green Roofs that look really pretty, filtering rain, growing plants, and cooling the city.

H is for Habitat, where creatures can thrive. Clean water, food, and shelter will keep you alive.

POLLINATORS WELCOME HERE!

Certified Wildlife Habitat

is for infiltration, rain soaking into the ground; replenishing aquifers and helping soil life abound.

J is for Joy when you look under a log, discovering a salamander, a toad, or a frog.

K is for Kids, exploring their streams, playing in the water, which is nice and clean.

L is for Living shoreline, littoral edge; stabilized by aquatic grasses and many kinds of sedge.

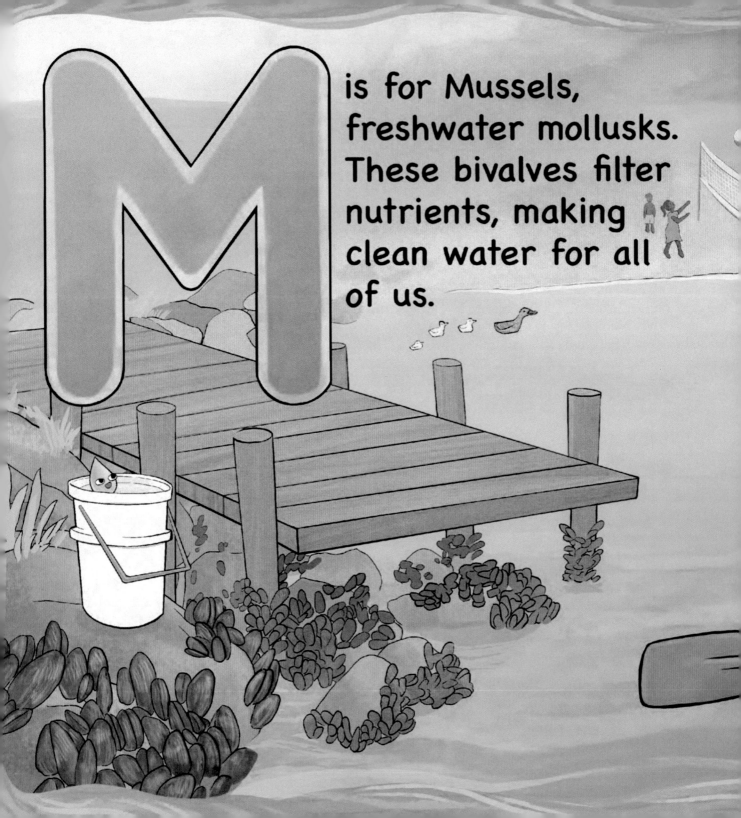

M is for Mussels, freshwater mollusks. These bivalves filter nutrients, making clean water for all of us.

N is for Nitrogen that makes the plants grow, but too much and it runs off in stormwater flow.

is for Ocean, with currents and tides, cycling Earth's water from surface to sky.

P is for Plants, home in wetlands and dry, feeding hungry pollinators as they fly or flutter by.

Q is for Quality of water we drink, clean water for all in both streams and the sink!

R is for Riparian buffers around streams, trees and shrubs keep the water cool and clean.

S is for Snow, flaky and deep. It melts into the ground and comes out in seeps.

T is for Tributaries, winding through the trees, sending water to the rivers in the heat and in the freeze.

is for Upstream waters that flow, linking people to neighbors that live down below.

W is for Watersheds, some big and some small; water flows off the ridges to streams and waterfalls.

X is for Xylem that flows in the trees, transporting water from roots to the leaves.

Y is for You, and all other creatures, that share the need for clean water and want to enjoy all its features.

Z is for Zooplankton, grazing away, at the base of the food chain, they support us each day.

Now we have learned an ABC
Water from aquifers,
For you and for me,
Water in streams,
And places we play
Let's keep water clean,
Do your part today.

Vocabulary

- **aquifer**–a layer of underground water-bearing permeable rock and soil from which groundwater wells (essential human access to healthy water) are drilled.

- **benthic macroinvertebrate**—small, benthic ("bottom-dwelling") organisms, such as dragonfly larvae and shrimp, that lack a backbone and are visible without the aid of a microscope. Scientists use the abundance, variety, and overall health of benthic macroinvertebrates as indicators when evaluating the quality of water.

- **conservation landscape**—a collaborative approach to creating and maintaining landscapes that prioritize supporting native soils by using native plant communities endemic (native) to a given area or region, and establishing a healthy ecosystem at the site level.

- **downpour**—a large amount of rainfall in a short period of time.

- **estuary**—a partially enclosed body of brackish water (where freshwater and saltwater intermix) typified by grassy vegetation and tidal activities. Estuaries are sensitive bodies of water that provide rich nurseries for fish and other organisms. Upstream pollution, containing harmful sediments and chemicals, can foul the nutrient sources in estuaries, causing damage to the estuary habitats.

- **fish**—gilled bony aquatic organisms with brains and no limbs.

- **green roof**—a vegetated roof designed as a system that sits on a building's structural waterproof roof and filters water, supports plants, and cools the air directly over the roof.

- **habitat**—a place which supports the life within it.

- **infiltration**—the process of a liquid, such as water, moving into and soaking into another medium, such as soil.

- **joy**—a happy expression often made by people when they are delighted with something.

- **kids**—young children or baby goats; used in reference to young people in the context of this book.

- **littoral zone**—also known as the littoral edge or nearshore; the area of a sea, lake or river which is close to the shore and permanently submerged. https://kids.kiddle.co/Littoral_zone

- **living shoreline**—shorelines that support life on the edge of water. Shoreline grasses and other plants create still zones which are ideal for nurturing baby aquatic animals.

- **mussel**—a type of bivalve mollusk benthic macroinvertebrate that is a filter feeder (bivalves are a large class of mollusks) https://kids.kiddle.co/Bivalve

- **nitrogen**—a nutrient that promotes green growth. Too much nitrogen in water causes overgrowth. In the atmosphere it forms nitrogen dioxide, which happens when fossil fuels are burned. When combined with rainfall, it creates acid rain which is harmful to plants and waterways. https://www.epa.gov/no2-pollution/basic-information-about-n02

- **ocean**—the majority of the Earth is covered with salt water that is found in oceans. The seven oceans are: North Pacific, South Pacific, North Atlantic, South Atlantic, Antarctic, Arctic, Indian. https://en.wikipedia.org/wiki/Seven_Seas

- **plants**—cellular organisms that appeared eons ago on Earth that developed from algae into terrestrial organisms able to make their own food. The Devonian period is when plants began to extensively colonize land; land animals followed the plants. *https://biologydictionary.net/plant/* *https://paleontologyworld.com/exploring-prehistoric-life-prehistoric-flora-fauna/devonian-period-climate-animals-plants*

- **quality**—a term used to evaluate and quantify the essential nature of a substance. There is a purity standard for water; references to water quality compare water samples to that standard. High quality fresh water (water with no pollution) is necessary for life.

- **riparian buffer**—a zone of land adjacent to a stream or river that is planted with the intent of protecting water quality. Riparian buffer plantings rely on native species that shade the waterway.

- **snow and seep**—snow is frozen water in the form of crystallized flakes that fall from the sky. Seeps are moist places on the earth's surface where water that has infiltrated the groundwater or interflow oozes out from an aquifer. In winter, the seeps (which drip or pool in warm weather) may freeze. This creates frozen pool mud, which is used by some species for hibernation, and may create icicles on rock surfaces.

- **tributary**—a freshwater stream feeding a larger stream, river, or lake, known as a mainstem. Tributaries form networks that appear similar to the vein growth patterns found on leaves.

- **upstream**—in or towards the higher part of a stream; against the current.

- **vernal pool**—a seasonal body of water that forms in the vernal (spring) warmer months from melting snow and other runoff that dries out completely in summer and is typically refilled during autumn. parts of a stream system that form in the vernal period (spring). Vernal pools provide important breeding habitat for many terrestrial and semiaquatic species, including spring peepers and chorus frogs.

- **watershed**—an area defined by a series of high points, such as hills or mountains, that channels rainfall, snowmelt, and waterways downhill to streams, rivers, and lakes and eventually to outflow points such as reservoirs, oceans, and bays. Watersheds often have subwatersheds that create a nested system of smaller water systems.

• **xylem**—a type of tissue that transports water soluble nutrients in vascular plants (such as ferns, trees, mosses, and flowering plants). Maple syrup is made from the xylem of maple trees.
https://en.wikipedia.org/wiki/Sylem
https://botanistinthekitchen.blog/2013/03/18/maple-syrup-mechanics/

• **you**—a reminder that water quality is impacted by you. You have the ability—and responsibility—to protect the water quality of the earth. You can contribute to healthier water quality by not littering, picking up pet waste, reducing water-wasting lawns, avoiding excessive fertilizers and pesticides, and supporting soil health with composted leaves and plantings of native plants. We can all enjoy healthy habitats by protecting our sources of high-quality water.

• **zooplankton**—microscopic aquatic organisms found in freshwater, oceans, and seas that are crucial to maintaining healthy water temperature, chemical balance, and life-supporting energy.

About the Author

Ann English is a landscape architect with a life-long love of plants and nature. She spent many happy hours outside exploring local ponds and streams when she was growing up and continued that in her professional life. She is a designer and educator who focusses on restoring ecosystem function, often using plant based systems. Ann has degrees in American History/ Architectural History (BA, UPenn), Regional Planning (MRP, Penn State), and Landscape Architecture (MLA, UGA), has three grown children and two grandchildren and lives in Maryland with her husband Don and dog Murphy.

About the Illustrator

Clarissa Libertelli is a freelance artist born and raised in the DC area whose work often centers on environmental themes. Her illustrations have been featured in everything from children's books to community composting guides.

Made in the USA
Middletown, DE
11 February 2022

61002540R00022